Armando & María Rosa

Leidi

Don Victor & María Rosa

Doña Satulina

Tía Berta

Pyramid of the Magician at Uxmal

Mayeros

A YUCATEC MAYA FAMILY

Tío Elías & Alberto   Luís   Adela   Chichí   Abuelito

GEORGE ANCONA

LOTHROP, LEE & SHEPARD BOOKS   NEW YORK

The backgrounds here and on page 1 show
Mayan ruins at Uxmal.

To my children,

Lisa, Gina, Tomas, Isabel, Marina, Pablo,

con todo mi cariño

I should like to thank the people who helped make this book a reality: my cousins in Yucatán, Arturo and
Rosa Ofelia Peniche and José Ruy and Honoria Triáy Peniche, for their hospitality and help; William Brito
Sansores, native of Teabo and Maya linguist, who introduced me to Maestra Rosario Novelo Canché, mayor of
the town of Teabo, and reviewed and commented on the text; María Satulina Paat Caamal, her husband,
Victor Daniel Moo Moo, and their extended, warm, and hospitable family; Luís Isauro Comal Caamal, for
translating Maya into Spanish for me; and Gaspár, for carrying my equipment. Back home in Santa Fe, thanks
go to Josie Caruso, who shared her library, knowledge, and passion for Maya history with me; to Verne
Scarborough, for reviewing the manuscript; and to Susan Pearson, my editor, who encouraged me to make this
personal journey.

Muchísimas gracias.

Printed in Singapore   First Edition   1 2 3 4 5 6 7 8 9 10
Library of Congress Cataloging in Publication Data
Ancona, George. Mayeros: A Yucatec family / by George Ancona.   p.   cm. Summary: Text and photographs present the life and customs of the descendants
of the Maya now living in the Yucatan Peninsula area of Mexico. ISBN 0-688-13465-3. — ISBN 0-688-13466-1 (lib. bdg.) 1. Mayas—Social life and customs—
Juvenile literature. 2. Yucatan Peninsula—Social life and customs—Juvenile literature. 3. Mayas—Pictorial works—Juvenile literature. [1. Mayas—Social life
and customs. 2. Indians of Mexico—Social life and customs. 3. Yucatan (Mexico: State)—Social life and customs.]
1. Title. F1435.A627 1997 972'.6—dc20   96-2309 CIP AC

One of the earliest words I learned was *chichí*, the Mayan word for grandmother. My mother would tell me of my *chichí* who lived in Mexico, but I got to know her only through the letters she sent on my birthdays. It wasn't until I graduated from high school and traveled to Yucatán that I met her and discovered the warmth, humor, and dignity of the Mayan people.

My return to Yucatán to do this book has been a journey of rediscovery. The stories, foods, music, and jokes of my childhood home in Brooklyn, New York, were also present in the tiny town of Teabo. Visiting with the family of Armando and Gaspár was like returning to my childhood.

Doña Satulina, their mother, served *puchero*, the same chicken stew my mother served for Sunday dinners. I remembered my mother scrubbing clothes when I photographed Satulina doing the laundry in a *batea.* The dancers at the fiesta brought back memories of my parents dancing the *jarana* in our living room. So allow me to share with you my visit to the land of my ancestors, the land of the Yucatec Maya.

George Ancona, Santa Fe, NM

The sounds of hammering echo in the plaza of Teabo, a small town on the Yucatán Peninsula in Mexico. Armando and his little brother, Gaspár, scamper over an unfinished bullring, playing hide-and-seek with their friends. Their father, don Victor, and the other men of the village are building the bullring for next week's fiesta to honor the town's patron saint.

A few blocks from the plaza is the house where Armando and Gaspár live with their parents and baby sister, María Rosa. Their thirteen-year-old sister, Leidi, has gone off to work as a nanny in the city of Mérida. The house is oval, with a thatched roof, just like the house that is carved over the entrance to a temple in the ruins of Uxmal. Uxmal is one of the great stone cities that were abandoned by the ancient Maya. Armando and his family call themselves *Mayeros*: the people who speak the Mayan language.

REAR: Tía Berta, Armando, Adela
FRONT: Doña Satulina holding María Rosa, Gaspár, don Victor

In the morning, Armando's mother, doña Satulina, makes breakfast for the family. She prepares a hot, frothy chocolate drink by beating a cacao-and-cinnamon tablet together with hot water in a wooden beater called a *batidora*. The ancient Maya offered this drink to the Spanish when they arrived on the Yucatán Peninsula in 1527.

On weekdays after breakfast, don Victor rides his bicycle to work on the *milpa*, the field where he grows their food. With clean shirts and combed hair, the boys go off to

school. And doña Satulina begins her chores. First she hauls water from the well behind the house. Since there are no freshwater rivers in Yucatán, natural underground pools called *cenotes* provide the water they need. Doña Satulina washes clothes in a flat wooden tub called a *batea*. While the men are working on their *milpas*, many women earn money by sewing and embroidering *huipiles*, the traditional Mayan dress, and by weaving hammocks.

For centuries, Mayan women have used the same kind of stone *metate* to grind their corn and spices. Nowadays, though, they take their cooked maize to the mill by the plaza, where they chat and gossip while waiting their turn to grind their maize into dough for tortillas.

Maize is considered both a food and a spiritual source by the Maya. Legends say that the gods made the Mayan people from dough made from maize.

Doña Satulina grinds spices on a stone *metate*.

Photograph by Justin Kerr

An ancient Mayan dish showing a woman using a *metate*

Women take their maize to the mill.

Inside the mill, the women grind their maize into dough.

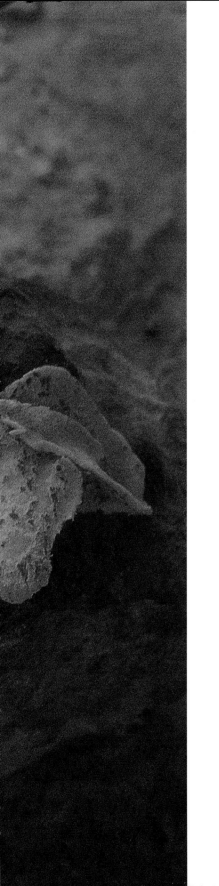

By midday, doña Satulina and her niece Adela are busy making tortillas for the family lunch, the *almuerzo,* which is the main meal of the day. Many Mexicans use the flat tortilla as both bread and as a spoon to scoop up their food.

At about two o'clock, don Victor, Armando, and Gaspár come home to eat. The Maya are very hospitable, and anyone who drops by is usually invited to stay for the meal.

ABOVE: Gaspár, Armando, María Rosa, & don Victor enjoy their lunch.
LEFT: Tortillas cooking on the *comal* LEFT INSERT: Doña Satulina and Adela making tortillas

After the *almuerzo,* hammocks are pulled down from the roof beams for everyone to rest and escape the midday heat. Since Yucatán is very hot, people find it cooler to sleep in the colorful string hammocks than in beds. Visitors are invited to spend the hot afternoon swaying, chatting, and napping.

When Spanish explorers arrived on the islands of the West Indies, they discovered that the native people slept in hammocks. Years later, when they landed on the shores of Yucatán, they introduced hammocks to the Maya.

Ancient Mayan calendar figure using a tumpline, from a carving on a stone monument in Copan, Honduras

In the late afternoon, when the heat of the day is over, the hammocks are put away and the town begins to stir again. Stores reopen and people go back to work.

Don Victor heads for the plaza. Every afternoon until the fiesta, he will be working on the bullring.

Using a tumpline, Armando fetches firewood. The ancient Maya did not have wheels or beasts of burden, so they used tumplines to carry goods over great distances.

Satulina and her sister-in-law Berta hire a young man with a tricycle to run errands around the town. Since school is over for the day, Gaspár goes along with them to get a haircut.

As evening approaches, the family returns home. Gaspár has been out playing and killed a *tusa,* a molelike animal. Tía Berta cooks it by burning and scraping off the fur, wrapping it in a banana leaf, and burying it under the coals of the kitchen fire until it is baked. The *tusa* is a delicacy they will eat for supper.

While doña Satulina makes tortillas, don Victor turns on the radio and the boys dance with Rosa. Only a few families in town have television.

After eating a light meal, the boys go to sleep. Their parents may weave, sew, or stroll over to the plaza to sit and chat with friends in the coolness of the evening. Gradually the hammocks fill the one-room house as each member of the family curls up for the night.

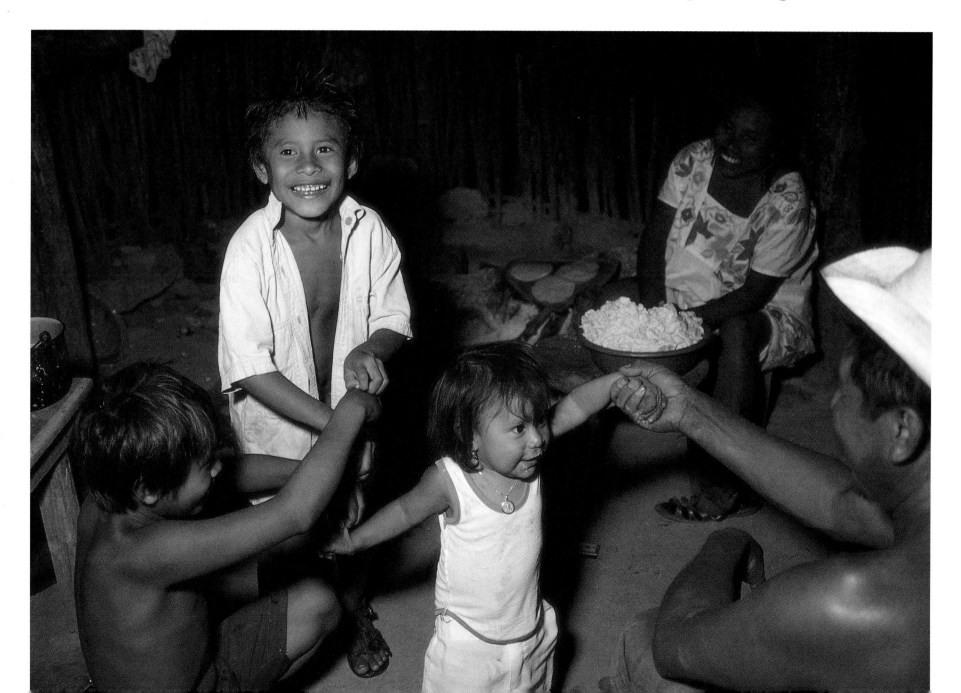

On Sunday, doña Satulina, tía Berta, and the children trek out to the family ranch and *milpa* to visit and bring fresh food back to town. Don Victor stays behind to work on the bullring, but they are joined by Leidi, who has been given time off from her job to return to Teabo for the fiesta.

They start early in the day. Shafts of sunlight pierce the canopy of leaves. Birds sing and insects buzz. Armando, Gaspár, and their cousin Jaime run ahead. The women follow, their babies on their hips.

Tía Berta stops to make a tumpline of her shawl, her *rebozo,* which makes it easier to carry her baby, Alberto. But when her older son, Luís, meets them on the path, Alberto gets a bike ride. Luís lives in town with his wife and baby but works on the ranch.

Ancient Mayan drawing of a dog, from the Madrid codex

The ranch is a cluster of houses near a huge ceiba tree. Leidi hides behind it to surprise the cousins. When she pops out, they all shout, *"¡La Xtabay! ¡La Xtabay!"* This is the name of the beautiful spirit woman who, according to legend, sits in the branches of the ceiba combing her hair and lures *milperos* to their death.

Armando and Gaspár's grandparents live on the ranch with other aunts, uncles, and cousins. The people who work or live on the ranch are isolated and speak only Maya among themselves. The women and children who stay in town all day speak mostly Spanish. Don Victor feels bad that Leidi no longer understands him.

The ranch dogs come to greet tía Berta,
doña Satulina, and María Rosa.

The ancient Maya hunted deer, tapir, monkeys, and wild turkey for meat. The Spanish introduced horses, cattle, pigs, and chickens to the New World. On the ranch, the family raises cattle for meat and milk. Armando gets on a horse to help lasso a steer for branding. The boys whoop and holler, and soon the steer is roped and on the ground. Luís burns a brand into the animal's hide.

The ancient Maya also cultivated bees in hollow logs for honey and wax. Today Yucatán is famous for its honey, which is exported to other countries. From a distance, the boys watch as Luís blows smoke into a hive to calm the bees so he can remove the honey.

Armando & Chichí

Abuelito trims a leaf from the henequen plant.

Armando visits with his *chichí,* his grandmother, who fell recently and hurt her wrist. Since she cannot walk to town, she is being treated at home by the family. Then his grandfather, his *abuelito,* shows him the old way of getting sisal hemp from a leaf of the henequen plant.

Then he crushes the pulp and juice from the leaf . . .

and ties the fibers together in preparation for weaving.

He uses a wooden rasp to crush out the pulp and juice until only the strands of sisal hemp remain. Abuelito will use these fibers to weave rope and twine. Before the invention of synthetic fibers, rope and twine were woven from sisal hemp, and Yucatán exported much of the world's supply.

The Mayan farmer believes that he borrows the land from the spirits of the forest. He will use the land for two years, and then return it to the forest and the creatures who live there.

Months ago, at the beginning of the dry season, the men cut a clearing in the forest to make a new *milpa.* They took the wood they needed for cooking and building and left the brush to dry. Now that the dry season is ending, the men and boys set fire to the brush. When the fire dies down, the ashes that are left will fertilize the thin layer of topsoil. The Maya have used this slash-and-burn method of farming for more than four thousand years.

In a few weeks, when the rains begin, don Elías will plant maize in the new *milpa* in the same way his ancestors did. With a pointed stick, he will poke a hole into the blackened earth. Then he will drop in a few kernels of maize and cover the seeds with his foot. He will also plant beans, squash, potatoes, pumpkins, chiles, melons, and spices among the maize.

Armando and Gaspár help their uncle Elías pick some maize and vegetables from the old *milpa* to bring back to the ranch.

Ancient Mayan drawing of a god using a planting stick to plant maize, from the Madrid codex

When they return to the ranch, the boys are put to work rubbing dry kernels off ears of maize. Then the kernels are soaked and cooked to soften them so that Satulina and Adela can grind them to make *atole,* a cool drink of cornmeal and water.

By now it is time to eat. The women serve an *almuerzo* of *puchero,* a tasty chicken stew. In ancient times, a wild turkey would have been used instead of the chicken. Three generations of men sit down to eat together. At the ranch, the women and younger children follow tradition and eat apart from them.

After the *almuerzo,* the children gather around Abuelito for a story. Then it is time to go. The boys kiss their grandparents and uncles good-bye and the family walks back to town, laden with fresh fruits and vegetables.

Detail of a drawing on an ancient vase showing a man drinking from a jícara like those used today

For the next few days, excitement over the upcoming fiesta rises. Amusement rides and food stands are set up in the plaza. At last the bullring is finished and the decorations are complete.

On the first day of the fiesta, doña Satulina leads a procession of *señoras,* the married women of the town. They carry flowers and candles to the church to place at the feet of their patron saint.

Men walk alongside them, shooting off rockets to announce that the fiesta has begun. For the next six days, there will be bullfights and dancing that will attract many people from nearby villages and towns.

Outside the bullring, refreshments are sold.

That evening, the entire family dresses in their best clothes and goes to the plaza. Musicians have come to town to play for the traditional dances called *jaranas.* The dances go on late into the night while fireworks light up the sky. Armando and Gaspár ride the carousel and roam among the crowds.

The next day, Friday, splendidly dressed dancers assemble under the portico of the town hall. Women and girls dress in beautifully embroidered white *huipiles* with *rebozos.* They wear flowers and ribbons in their hair and gold filigree earrings and necklaces. The men and boys wear white shirts called *guayaberas,* white pants, sandals, and straw hats. Men, women, boys, and girls all dance with one another.

The next four days are for the bullfights. *Vaqueros* lead the roped bulls through the streets to the bullring. The bullfighters come from the city to match their skill and bravery with those of the bulls. The crowds cheer and jeer both bulls and toreadors.

If a bull is brave and fights, the toreador kills him with a sword. The dead bull is butchered and the fresh meat is sold to the crowds outside the bullring.

Each night, Armando and Gaspár try to stay awake as long as possible to watch the dancers, games, and rides. But eventually the boys return home. Soon the hammocks rock in the quiet house and the family sleeps as the last strains of the *jaranas* echo in the night.

On Wednesday, life returns to its everyday rhythms. The fiesta is over. Grown-ups return to work; children go back to school. Armando and Gaspár's teachers are preparing them for the future by teaching them Spanish and the skills they will need to succeed in a fast-changing world. Working alongside their father, they will continue to speak Maya and may grow up to be *milperos* too, but they will also speak Spanish. Armando and Gaspár are the future Maya, a people with a rich heritage who are making a greater place for themselves in the fast-changing world.

Mayan scribe drawing on a codex, from a painting on an ancient vase

A Note from the Author

For four thousand years, since before national borders existed, the Maya have lived in what is now Yucatán and in the southern highlands of Mexico, Belize, Honduras, El Salvador, and Guatemala. Today there are two million Maya who speak twenty-four Mayan languages. The Yucatec Maya are called the Lowland Maya.

Armando and Gaspár's family are descendants of a great civilization, which reached its peak between 300 and 900 AD. During these centuries, they built great stone cities, some of which can be visited today. Others lie in ruins, hidden in the tangle of forest vines and trees.

About thirty miles from Teabo are the ruins of Uxmal, where Mayan kings and priests lived. Excavations show that around the pyramids and temples stood simple one-room houses like the one Armando and Gaspár live in today.

The ancient Maya developed a very accurate calendar and knew the paths of the stars and planets. They recorded their history in hieroglyphic writings painted on pottery, carved into their stone buildings, or written in books called codices. They believed that their rulers were living gods who could speak with the gods of nature. Dressed in elaborate armor and headdresses, these rulers led warriors into battle. The defeated became slaves of the victors or were sacrificed to the gods.

At some point, the great Mayan cities were mysteriously abandoned, and the forest covered them over. It is believed that warfare, overpopulation, famine, and plagues weakened the Mayan city-states. By the time the Spanish arrived in Yucatán in 1527, they had been abandoned, and it wasn't until 1842 that European explorers began to uncover the hidden ruins.

Feuds between the various peoples of Mexico made it easier for the Spanish to conquer them. It took Cortez only two years to conquer the Aztecs: Because of ancient prophecy, Moctezuma, the king of the Aztecs, believed the Spanish to be returning gods and welcomed them. The Maya did not believe this and resisted, and it was twenty years before the Maya of Yucatán were totally defeated.

With the conquistadors came missionary priests determined to convert the Maya to Christianity. Those who resisted were tortured or put to death. Believing that the Mayan codices were blasphemous, Bishop Diego de Landa burned all he could find, destroying thousands of years of Mayan history, science, and legend. Mayan history survives mainly through storytelling.

The Maya were made slaves, branded, and sold. They were put to work in gold, silver, copper, and mercury mines, or on haciendas raising sugar cane and henequen. With stones taken from the ruins of their ancient temples, they built great Spanish colonial churches.

When the Spanish began to have children with the Maya, a new caste was created called *mestizos*. To distinguish their caste, *mestiza* women's white *huipiles* were decorated with the elaborate embroidery seen at fiestas today.

When the first ruins of the great cities of the Maya were discovered 150 years ago, European scholars were astonished that such a highly developed civilization had existed in the western hemisphere before European colonization. Since then, archeologists have been painstakingly unearthing the remains of the stone cities. Bit by bit, the hieroglyphics in the temples and the few remaining codices are being deciphered.

For more than five hundred years, the Maya have been adapting their traditions to those the Spanish introduced, and vice versa. Today much of their religion, dress, food, music, and dance is a blend of ancient Mayan with Spanish traditions.

Statue of the plumed serpent at Chichen Itza

Glossary of Spanish and Yucatec Words

abuelito (ah-bway-LEE-toh): little grandfather, an endearment like granddaddy

almuerzo (ahl-MWAIR-so): lunch

atole (ah-TOH-lay): a drink prepared with cornmeal

batea (bah-TAY-ah): a washtub; a flat-bottomed boat

batidora (bah-tee-DOR-ah): a wooden beater

cenote (say-NOH-tay): natural underground reservoir

chichí (chee-CHEE): Mayan word for grandmother

comal (coh-MAHL): flat, earthenware pan; frying pan

con mucho cariño (kohn MOO-choh car-EEN-yoh): affectionately

don (dohn): a man's title of respect

doña (DOHN-yuh): a woman's title of respect

fiesta (FYACE-tah): feast, party, holiday

gracias (GRAHS-eyus): thank you

guayabera (gwah-yah-BARE-ah): loose-fitting man's shirt

hacienda (ah-SYAIN-dah): a farm or ranch

huipil (wee-PEEL): a loosely fitted dress

jarana (hah-RAH-nah): dance, typical Yucatec dance

jícara (HEE-kah-rah): a bowl made from the calabash gourd

Mérida (MAY-ree-dah): capital city of the state of Yucatán

mestizo (mace-TEE-soh): a person of mixed race

metate (may-TAH-tay): a stone used for grinding

milpa (MEEL-pah): a field where food is grown

milpero (meel-PAIR-oh): a farmer who works on a milpa

muchísimas gracias (moo-CHEE-see-mahs GRAHS-eyus): thank you very much

puchero (poo-CHAIR-oh): a meat and vegetable stew

rebozo (rray-BOH-soh): a shawl

señor (say-NYOR): gentleman, sir, mister

señora (say-NYOR-ah): lady, wife, missus

tía (TEE-ah): aunt

tío (TEE-oh): uncle

tortilla (tor-TEE-yuh): unleavened cornmeal pancake

tusa (TOO-sah): a mole-like animal

Uxmal (OOSH-mahl): one of the Mayan ruins in Yucatan

vaquero (bah-KAY-roh): cowboy

Xtabay (shtah-BYE): female character in Yucatec legend